CO-WRITING
A BOOK

COLLABORATION AND
CO-CREATION FOR WRITERS

J. Thorn & Joanna Penn

Co-writing a Book: Collaboration and Co-creation for Writers

First Print Edition (2017)
Copyright © J. Thorn and Joanna Penn
www.TheCreativePenn.com
www.JThorn.net

ISBN: 978-1-912105-92-2

Publisher: Curl Up Press

Requests to publish work from this book should be sent to:
joanna@CurlUpPress.com

Cover and Interior Design: JD Smith

www.CurlUpPress.com

Contents

Introduction

Co-writing can be an amazing experience when two minds come together to create something new in the world. Or it can be a painful process that ends in disaster!

So, who are we?

J. Thorn is a bestselling horror and dark fantasy writer, co-founder of Molten Universe Media and a podcaster. He has worked in a number of collaborations, including a ten-author story and a post-apocalyptic series.

Joanna is a New York Times and USA Today bestselling thriller author (as J.F.Penn), blogger and podcaster at TheCreativePenn.com, award-winning entrepreneur, professional speaker, and author of non-fiction. Until she met J., Joanna considered co-writing just a little outside her comfort zone due to control-freakish tendencies

In 2015, we co-wrote *Risen Gods*, a dark fantasy thriller set in New Zealand. The first draft took us 19 days, proof that two can achieve great things. The result is a mind-meld between a couple of very different authors and the book gets great reviews from readers.

In 2017, we collaborated again on *American Demon Hunters: Sacrifice*, along with two other authors, Lindsay Buroker and Zach Bohannon. The four of us boarded the Amtrak train in Chicago to New Orleans and wrote a dark fantasy story in a week of writing and story meetings together. It was … intense.

In this book, we share our tips on how to successfully co-write a book and avoid the pitfalls along the way. We also include excerpts from our private co-writing diary, honest notes written every day that we used to communicate, plus quotes from interviews with our co-writers. We hope that this will help you with your own collaboration journey.

We also had a no-holds barred discussion about the co-writing process, which you can watch or listen to, or even read the transcript:

www.TheCreativePenn.com/cowriting-thorn-penn

1. What is co-writing?

Co-writing is essentially writing something with another person and is common in the publishing industry through different models. For example,

- **Big name authors who co-write with 'lesser known' authors** e.g. James Patterson with Maxine Paetro, and many others. This model has proved popular and expanded to many of the top-selling authors e.g. Clive Cussler and Janet Evanovitch

- **Authors who regularly write as a pair and separately** e.g. Douglas Preston & Lincoln Child, and in the indie world, Bella Andre & Melissa Foster

- **Authors who write together but use one name** e.g. Nicci French, a crime writer who is actually the husband and wife team, Nicci Gerrard and Sean French

When co-writing together, there are a number of ways that the author roles can work:

(1) Each author takes a completely separate role

Assuming a distinction between the drafting and the revising process, authors can collaborate by taking different roles in the co-writing process. For example, in *Shadow Witch*, J. Thorn created a general outline, Dan Padavona wrote the first draft and J. Thorn revised. This is similar to the model that James Patterson uses with his co-writers. If both authors can recognize their preferred tendencies in the writing process and team up accordingly, taking separate roles allows them both to play to their strengths.

We did a version of this in *American Demon Hunters: Sacrifice*, where each of the four authors wrote a separate character, maintaining their individual voice, even as the story progressed together. More specific details in Chapter 12.

(2) One author acts as the 'conductor'

This process is suitable for a multi-author project and was used by J. Thorn in *The Black Fang Betrayal*, a ten-author collaborative story. One author, the conductor, takes the lead and outlines the entire story, then sends individualized prompts to the other writers. When they send their scenes back, the lead author fits them into the global story. J. goes into more detail about his lessons learned and tips for managing so many authors in Chapter 11.

(3) A/B drafting and revising

A/B drafting and revising is the co-writing process where each writer 'takes turns.' This can be by scene or chapter and it can be done in a non-linear fashion. Each author is actively writing the first draft, and a common method for this is passing the baton, or writing in an A/B fashion. Then, revisions can be done the same way; one author making a 'pass' and then giving it to the other author to do the same.

This was the method we used to write *Risen Gods*. It was made easier by the time difference between London and Ohio, as Joanna would write in the morning and finish her words before J. got up and did his.

2. Benefits of co-writing

There are a number of benefits to co-writing that make it well worth trying.

(1) Two (or more) heads are creatively better than one

Joanna was skeptical about co-writing for years, and many indie authors are on the high end of the control freak spectrum. That's why we're indies!

But then she did the online James Patterson writing masterclass and he talked about some of the greatest creative collaborations. His most memorable example was John Lennon and Paul McCartney, and Joanna was convinced it was worth a try. Sometimes two people can create something really amazing and unique, so it's worth the risk to see what you can do together.

(2) Fun and partnership

Collaboration is fun. There's a healthy, positive feedback loop when you co-create art, because you're in it together. Let's face it, most of our spouses, family and friends don't 'get' our writing. Once we've written a number of books, they're not even that interested in the latest project. Therefore, being able to share the excitement of a new plot twist or cover mock-up with your co-creator can be exciting and writing is no longer a solitary process. You also get to share the financial rewards, the excitement of publication and the ups and downs of the reviews over time.

This level of fun was even more apparent in the four author collaboration we did in New Orleans. Although we all identify as introverts, we enjoyed spending time talking about writing over story meetings, Creole dinners and even cultural outings like the Museum of Death. Let's face it, you can't take your Mom or your non-writer friends there!

(3) Sharing the workload

Yes, you only have to do half the number of words! Or even fewer if you have more writers.

We finished the first draft of *Risen Gods* in 19 days, which was a first for both of us in terms of speed. It was a rush to see the words piling up every day and addictive to see how far we could get together. We shared the editing and production aspects, and we made joint decisions about the map for the front of the book and the book cover. Writing and publishing a book as an indie author is hard work, so sharing the load can make it a whole lot easier.

For *Sacrifice*, we finished the first draft in a week between the four of us.

(4) Accountability

You know those days when you really don't feel like writing? You're tired and grumpy and your brain is fuzzy. You're busy at work, the family needs your attention and the last thing you want to do is put fingers to keyboard.

If you know that someone will be waiting for your words later that day, you find yourself pushing through, no matter how you feel. If you have a day off, you feel guilty because the other person is still pulling their weight. The real-life correlation is a workout partner or exercise buddy. When someone else is counting on you to show up so you can exercise together, you are less likely to stay home.

> "I've valued the accountability of only having a limited time. The hard deadline of everyone leaving and moving onto other projects. I was so paranoid that I would be behind with my words this week, but actually, because of jet-lag from UK time, I've ended up being ahead most of the week because I was up earlier." - J.F.Penn on *American Demon Hunters: Sacrifice*

(5) Creative challenge

Our job as writers is the work of a lifetime. Pushing ourselves creatively and personally is just part of the journey, and co-writing can challenge us in many different ways. When co-writing, you will most likely write outside your comfort zone, you will push yourself and you will have to compromise. This will help you grow as a person and as a creative, something we all need over time to sustain a long-term creative career.

(6) Finding new readers

If you co-write with someone in a similar genre to you, or slightly tangential to it, then you are likely to cross-pollinate your readers as some may try your other work. This will grow your own marketing platform and email list over time, which is a benefit to the authors involved, and to readers.

3. The difficulties of co-writing

While it can be an amazing creative experience to co-write a book, there are also likely to be difficulties along the way. Here are some of the issues that may come up.

(1) Anxiety and vulnerability

It is impossible to co-write without some degree of vulnerability. You have to let another artist into your process, often at a place where it's unpolished or unrefined, such as sharing a rough first draft. It can leave you feeling stilted and awkward, but that will subside the more you co-write, and it can fade quickly if you trust your writing partner.

If one author has more experience with collaborations, that person can also ease anxieties by sharing past experiences or times when they were in that same situation. J. did this for Joanna in the early days, when she was most worried about sharing first draft material, which, let's face it, is quite an intimate experience for a writer!

(2) Fear of judgment and comparisonitis

Other issues or feelings that can be triggered in a co-writing project are fear of judgment, 'comparisonitis' (comparing your writing to someone else's, often in a negative, self-judging fashion) or questions of self-worth.

If you're sharing that first draft, you may feel the fear of judgment for your ideas. Joanna has written more about this in *The Successful Author Mindset: A Handbook for Surviving the Writer's Journey.*

(3) Egomania and control freakery

Egomania or 'control freakery' is the desire to dominate the collaboration without consideration of your partner. It's possible that one person will be the dominant partner in terms of driving the story, but throughout all anxiety and adversity, it is important to be honest and open with your partner and to persevere if you can. Joanna certainly skated the edge of this during the process, but made sure to always ask J.'s permission to cut scenes and rewrite chapters.

Compromising a specific artistic vision can be difficult for some writers, and if you are really set on a certain way of doing things, co-writing will be a challenge. Co-writing is not for everyone, and if you hold on to a fixed idea of what the final outcome is going to be, you'll be disappointed, because it's not going to be that way.

Even if you're the one leading the project, it won't be what you think it's going to be when you begin. If you have control freak tendencies—and we all do—it will take a period of adjustment. Compromise is key when co-creating any kind of art. Having a prior trusting relationship with your co-writer can often help you to get past those moments of doubt.

(4) Risk

There will always be risk involved in any kind of multi-author collaboration, and there will always be things that you can't control. There's a financial risk, as you are investing time and money for editing, cover design, marketing, etc., when the project may never even make it commercially.

There's a time and opportunity cost risk. We all have a certain amount of time to write, and we all have to choose what we spend that time on. If you work on a collaboration, you will have less time to work on your own projects.

There's also the risk that your core readers won't want to read a collaboration and you have missed the chance to serve them with something they would buy.

Of course, you can't possibly come up with a contingency for every single one of these, so at some point you jump in and do it and figure out how to fix things later if they break.

4. Finding the right person to co-write with

We're all different people, so we will all find different types of collaboration partners. However, identifying the right partner is not always an easy task.

> "You can't have too many alpha dogs. I will go out on a limb, and without any scientific evidence, I would say it's probably more personality-based than work style-based. I think knowing who the people are and what they bring will trump the work style. You don't necessarily want all of the same type of people who work all the same way. But you don't want them to be radically different either. Or else, you won't get anything done. It's a balance." - J. Thorn, on *American Demon Hunters: Sacrifice*

Here are some elements that might help in finding the right person.

(1) Choose someone you can trust

Having a prior relationship can often give the project the best chance at success, although nothing is a guarantee. Because the professional relationship will last for 70 years beyond the lifespan of the authors (international copyright law), the partnership will last longer than a marriage. That means the project is a commitment that involves a high level of trust, as both authors jointly share in the royalties and the intellectual property.

"When I considered co-writing for the first time, J. was the only person who came to mind. His easy-going character and his experience in collaboration made him a great partner. Even though we've never met physically and live on separate continents, we've had years of online Skype calls and emails. I trust him and that's ultimately been the most important thing." *J.F.Penn*

(2) Choose someone with a similar level of writing experience

Although it's not impossible to collaborate as a new writer, there are some compelling reasons to establish your own voice and process before trying to do so with another writer. Fully developing your own writing voice and style can take time. It is difficult to co-write with another author before you know and understand yourself.

(3) Choose someone with a similar author brand

Although the two writers do not have to write in the exactly same genre, they should at least be compatible, so as to not alienate readers. For example, action adventure and thrillers would appeal to the same reader whereas horror and romantic fiction might not. Each writer will most likely have to 'move' closer to the common ground between the genres if they are not in the same genre.

(4) Choose someone with a comparable author platform

A big part of collaboration is marketing the finished work, so maturity of author platform is also a consideration when choosing a partner. Having two authors with roughly the same platform development (reach, readership, size of mailing list, etc.) can help create a common goal for the project with realistic expectations.

In addition, leveraging two author platforms to launch a single, shared title can amplify the success of the launch as well as the total available market of readers. There is a common language amongst authors who share the same platforms which helps to streamline the process.

(5) Choose someone who will complement your writing style

This was the first time that J. had collaborated with a female author, and we did find some gender differences when writing. Of course, there are differences of style and voice between any pair of authors and this should not prevent or hinder a collaboration.

Regardless of gender, recognizing those differences can help to unify the voice of the story. The important idea is to grow as a storyteller and incorporate what you've learned into future writing projects. Being deliberate about which author will write specific scenes or characters is another way of using stylistic differences to your advantage. In *Risen Gods*, J. primarily wrote the male protagonist's point of view, and Joanna wrote the female, although towards the end, we swapped roles and Joanna did the bulk of the male character's edits. It would be interesting to discover whether readers could tell the difference between the writing in the finished product.

"Collaborating is just like any other relationship. You don't force yourself to find the right person. It'll happen organically the more you network with other authors and eventually, if you're interested in co-authoring, you'll come across somebody that you mesh with." Zach Bohannon, on *American Demon Hunters: Sacrifice*

5. Before you start: Written legal agreement

Disclaimer: This is not legal advice. We are not attorneys/lawyers. This is just our opinion and experience.

Why do you need an agreement in place before writing?

The copyright on a book is usually 50-70 years after the death of the author, depending on the country you publish in. So if you co-write a book, you will be joined with this person for the rest of your life and for the future management of your intellectual property estate. This is longer than a marriage!

Of course, most of us don't consider that our books will make that much money, so this seems rather grandiose. But what if your book is the next *Da Vinci Code* or *Twilight* or *The Martian*? What if there are translation rights, film rights or a TV adaptation? You have to plan for possible success as well as possible failure and cover both options in your agreement.

In addition, discussing these things and making decisions at the outset of the collaboration can help to define non-writing roles. For example, who will publish the book? How will expenses be covered? How and when will royalties be dispersed? How often will sales reporting be done? At the time of this writing, it is not possible to use any major retailer's platform for a royalty-split project. In other words, one person will have to handle the publication and then be accountable to the other.

You also need to discuss what will happen if the project doesn't get to publication? Who owns the idea and the words written? Can one person take the idea and write a standalone? It's best to get on Skype and discuss these things before you start the first draft, just so everyone is clear.

For a legal standpoint on co-writing, check out *The Self-Publisher's Legal Handbook* by Helen Sedwick, which has a chapter on collaboration. See Appendix 1 for J. Thorn's example agreement that we used as the basis for *Risen Gods*.

Do you need a lawyer/attorney to do the agreement?

The legal implications of any collaboration should not be taken lightly, and consulting an attorney prior to drafting an agreement can be beneficial for both parties. However, if there is trust in place then you can opt to do your own written agreement which you both sign once complete.

You should *definitely* do a written agreement, regardless of your relationship with the co-writing partner. This enables you to cover all the possibilities upfront. Hopefully nothing will go wrong, but if it does, you know how it will work.

We decided to do a written agreement that we both signed without the need for an attorney and you'll find an example in Appendix 1. We used Docracy.com for electronically signing and filing.

What should the agreement cover?

If the co-writing project is going to be an equal partnership, the arrangement can be kept quite simple. Here's what we agreed for *Risen Gods*:

- 50/50% split on everything – the time spent in writing and editing, costs of production and marketing and the income

- Copyright would be jointly held between J.F.Penn and J. Thorn

- Any rights associated with the book would also be split e.g. audio book, film, merchandising

- The world of the book, including characters, is jointly owned and we would need to consult with the other before writing in it again. We could co-write together in the world, or write our own books in the world, but co-writing with someone else in the world would require a further agreement

For *American Demon Hunters: Sacrifice*, the copyright is jointly held between the four of us for this book, with royalties equally split between us. But as the book is written in one of J.'s existing worlds, the other three authors have no right to continue writing in the world without J.'s permission.

Long-term collaborators often have a legal company structure in place for their co-written works and publication is done under that umbrella, for example, Sterling & Stone publishes works by Sean Platt, co-writing with Johnny B Truant, and co-writing separately with David Wright. For smaller projects, one author needs to be the one to publish the book and do the associated distribution as well as the royalty split and payments over time. For *Risen Gods*, Joanna took on the publisher role and J. took it on for *Sacrifice*.

6. Practicalities and process

The process of co-writing adds more complexity to writing a book on your own. Here are the main aspects.

(1) Structure, plan and plot your book in advance

You need something for both parties to work from in order to progress the work. This may be an outline and/or story beats for fiction, or a chapter/topic outline for non-fiction.

Being explicitly clear about the creative direction of the project will help to make sure that non-negotiable situations are avoided. Having a detailed outline or story arc can go a long way in making sure both writers understand where the story will go and how to get it there.

As *Risen Gods* was Joanna's idea, she provided a story outline using Shawn Coyne's book *The Story Grid*. This provided some of the high points of the book, including the beginning and the end, but it needed to be more detailed. J. was left hanging for some scenes, and we had to spend more time in editing because we didn't plan enough up front. Extensive plotting in pre-production would have helped prevent wasted scenes that were later cut or changed.

For *Sacrifice*, we have to admit to ignoring our own advice, attempting to proceed without a clear outline because of the time constraints. The story problems we had between the four authors came down to missing this step, as you can read in Chapter 12. So do what we say, don't do what we do!

> "If I did another collaboration in the future, I'd probably want an outline from day one. I'm fine with outlines being flexible and people doing their own things, but I think when you're doing this with four people, it's super helpful if you know where your character needs to be at different points in the story. That was probably the hurdle for me. And once we did do that outline, I've been a lot more comfortable." - Lindsay Buroker, on *American Demon Hunters: Sacrifice*

(2) Agree your dates for starting the writing, editing and publication

Creating a production schedule is essential to hitting deadlines and avoiding delays. Of course, 'real life' gets in the way of everyone's book projects, but when there's two (or more) people involved, you have to make sure you coordinate timing.

We had to postpone the start of *Risen Gods* due to clashes with other projects, but then we nailed down a start date and a rough finish date before beginning. Once finally agreed, we met our deadlines. You also need to allow for each other's speed of writing. We aimed for 1,500 words each per day, sometimes exceeding that and other days writing under. It just depended on the scene and it all equaled out in the end.

The dates for the first draft of *Sacrifice* were constrained by actually meeting in person to get on the train on a Sunday night, arriving in New Orleans on Monday and then leaving the following Saturday with a tight editing and production timeline. We went from zero to published book in one month. This is definitely a hard-core way to arrange things, but it's also creatively satisfying.

(3) Coordinating the writing

Various tools exist to make co-writing easier. They range from the exchanging of Microsoft Word documents, to collaborating in real time with Google Drive documents or a Scrivener project shared on DropBox.

There is no 'one' tool or 'right' tool for co-writing. Scrivener is a favorite of writers because the program contains so many additional functions that help to organize the manuscript and go beyond simple word processing, such as document notes, tags and an elegant corkboard organization tool. Combining the power of Scrivener with the versatility of DropBox can create a powerful and simple co-writing environment. Although we used Google Drive documents for this project, we would use Scrivener with DropBox in the future to allow for the extended Inspector functionality that we used in editing.

Keeping a word count journal can be motivating. Using something as simple as a spreadsheet, each writer can log word count for the day, and seeing the word count add up faster than they would if you were writing alone can be incredibly motivating. Our first draft for *Risen Gods* was written in an AB-AB pattern, alternating the writing of scenes and chapters even if they were not written in a linear fashion.

(4) Communication before, during and after

It is critical to communicate with your co-writer. Without this, the project is very likely to fail. Regular communication can help keep things on task, whether that be via email, a shared journal document, Skype or video chats – even face-to-face meetings if you want. This communication allows for meta-cognitive reflection as well as creating a side-stream conversation about the story and the process which helps keep both parties informed.

For *Risen Gods*, we used a shared Google Doc to write daily notes to each other instead of using email, and included story and character notes as well as emotional reactions. This helped to keep the creation aspect separate from the practical things like cover design. You can read some of our notes in Chapter 7, to get an idea of how the process worked.

Honesty is definitely the best policy here. Just share if you're feeling like you're under too much pressure, or if you feel that the other person is not doing enough. Talking about it sooner rather than later is the best way forward. Of course, 'talking' doesn't have to mean actually speaking. We didn't 'talk' at all after the initial agreement!

(5) Editing, proofreading, cover design, production and marketing tasks

One author needs to be at the end of the production line making final decisions about the project. This extends through the editing process into decisions about proofreading, formatting, cover design and the book's product page. Obviously, collaboration should be done here but ultimately, you have to decide where the buck stops.

Editing was difficult for us, as we both have very different processes. Joanna spends more time in first draft writing, circling through the manuscript and then does fewer edits. J. does a very rough first draft and then cycles through a lot more, taking more time on editing. We hadn't discussed this upfront, making assumptions that we were similar. *[Tip: Don't assume anything!]*

J. found the revision process challenging because he had followed the Stephen King approach from *On Writing*, setting a draft aside for three months to let the story simmer. J. normally takes drafts through five or six revisions over several months, each time printing out the book and sitting down with a red pen to go through the whole thing. He would then take it back to the computer, make changes, print it out and do it again. Between each one of those, he would let it sit while writing short stories or working on different projects. This would allow him to let the story percolate and think about what he wanted to do in the next round of revisions. In this project, J. had to condense that process into eight days. He admits to procrastinating, feeling overwhelmed by the challenge – but being held accountable to Joanna meant he had to get started. J. spent an entire weekend, 14 hours each day, working on it and he felt a sense of accomplishment in being able to do in 2 days what would normally take him months.

> "When you're talking about a running collaboration, the ability to preserve what's unique about your voice, but also at the same time to create a cohesive experience for the reader, that's what we're all chasing. I just do my best, and I learn every time." - J. Thorn, on *American Demon Hunters: Sacrifice*

Joanna did an edit of the entire manuscript of *Risen Gods* in order to make the voice consistent throughout the story.

She acknowledged the difficulty of that revision because she had to make decisions on selections of the text that J. had written and synthesize the voice, while adding a layer that would bring the story together. Several edits went back and forth before the manuscript was sent to the professional editor for a global story edit and a line edit.

We used Joanna's editor and proofreader. We also had two specialist beta readers to cover the Maori cultural aspects and vulcanology. We also used Joanna's cover designer, and Joanna published the book through her distribution accounts. She is responsible for dispersing royalties over the long term. Marketing will continue to be a joint responsibility.

(6) Managing the on-going relationship

Once the book is out there, you still have to maintain your relationship over time. One partner will manage the publication process and therefore will receive money into their bank account. This needs to be dispersed and also documented so both partners can keep their accounts in order. Joanna will be maintaining a Google Doc with monthly sales and will do a royalty statement on payment. For multi-national payments, PayPal or international money transfer are the easiest way to do transfers.

There may be discussion over pricing and promotions over time, and opportunities like putting the book into a multi-author boxset or competition. So don't just write and run! Arrange how you will continue the relationship into the future, even if you're not planning to write together again.

7. Excerpts from our Risen Gods co-writing diary

During the process of writing *Risen Gods*, we kept a Google Doc on a shared drive and wrote in it every day. Before we started writing for the day, we checked the document and read the notes from the other. We didn't speak during the process, but keeping our thoughts and feelings in writing made daily communication easy, especially as we were writing in different time zones.

7 Sep - J.F.Penn

I'm definitely feeling more stilted in my first draft. The thought of someone else reading my first draft words is making me self-edit more, which slows my writing down. I need to stop doing this and trust the process. I find myself even looking at repetitive words in the thesaurus already, and I'm not even 200 words in. Need to censor the self-edit!

7 Sep - J. Thorn

I've gotten over that feeling of first-draft exposure because I've done this before. However, not knowing New Zealand and with only a crash-course on Maori is going to slow me down... That being said, I have HUGE insecurity issues writing with you, and that will be my challenge. I know once we get a few thousand words in, we'll both be much more comfortable, but I have anxiety around my ability to write to your level.

I'll most likely read but not edit your stuff, but feel free to do whatever you need to do to mine. As the 'lead' in this, I think you should probably light-touch my stuff to closer match your voice. I tend to revise a ton, so my first draft stuff is raw. Give yourself permission to not self-edit. Only you and I are seeing this and we're equally vulnerable. The finished version will be outstanding so let's take the first-draft pressure off of ourselves.

8 Sept - J. Thorn

When I was a kid, I played these quest video games. You could see a small map in the corner but it was all black. As you moved through the maze, the map appeared as if a spotlight followed your character. That's kind of how I feel in this (which is good). I sense you have the map – or at least an idea for it – and when you leave me specifics to write, it frees me up from trying to fit that localized scene into the bigger picture. This is a long-winded way of saying I like how our process is developing. I have no problem with you telling me which chapters need written. Every collab is so different. This is the first time I've been more of the follower and I'm really enjoying it!

9 Sept - J. Thorn

You have a very cinematic style in your draft whereas I'm more minimalist. I'm trying to include more setting and details in my scenes to bring them closer together and hopefully minimize lots of editing later. Feel free to push me in one direction or another… It's very different writing with someone than reading their stuff, isn't it?

14 Sept - J. Thorn

Our first documented moment of 'collaboration magic!' I wrote Chapter 12 before I read your Chapter 11... Awesome!

15 Sept - J. Thorn

Almost 21k words now ;) I can feel the storylines converging. Really awesome... I seriously have no ego about what I write. I just want to make the best story possible.

16 Sept - J.F.Penn

In terms of reflection on our writing style, it will be interesting to see how we knit this together in the final edits, as we are quite different – have you co-authored with a woman before? Or am I the first? I do find your writing masculine – whatever that means.

16 Sept - J. Thorn

I have not co-authored with a woman. I also did some poking around and I think male/female collabs are quite rare, so kudos to us for doing it. I'm confident we'll end with something really good. I would also add that being in bands for 20 years and then doing co-writing projects has made this type of work easier for me. Writing songs is entirely collaborative and the band members always have to knit the song elements together into a cohesive whole. I totally understand where you are and that this is your first collab. I trust you and the process, and I know we'll have something great. Collabs always feel awkward at times.

17 Sept - J.F.Penn

I am enjoying the movement of the story between us and the additional word count every day – that's awesome… I realize that I've taken primary on the initial story idea this time around, so would be interested to see what would happen when you took the story lead…but just wanted to say that it's all good so far!

17 Sept - J. Thorn

I'm seriously loving this, Jo. Having to write in this world/ mythology that is not native to me is making me a better writer. I can feel it… While not nuanced or polished, we're knocking out thousands of quality words each day. I feel like we have a rhythm.

18 Sept - J.F.Penn

I'm glad you think the process is productive and smooth. I have nothing to compare it to. But I very much like the accountability of alternating writing. It makes it 'easier' to sit down and do the words, knowing you're coming in later and doing yours.

22 Sept - J. Thorn

Having those chapter targets is SO helpful. I feel like I can now see the light at the end of the tunnel… I eked out 1500 words today but I struggled. I tried writing the kayak scene but I was a… fish out of water. Ha! Seriously, I couldn't quite nail it so I left brackets at two places in the chapter. I can take a crack at it in revisions or you can add it in later. Either way is fine. I could have spent some time researching it, but was afraid I'd lose my momentum so I pushed on.

23 Sept - J. Thorn

I've always found the best partnerships come from an aligned purpose but with slightly different strengths. You sensed my struggle with the authenticity of that scene even before I could articulate it. I NEVER could have written such an incredible kayak scene. Thank you for taking that burden off my shoulders.

23 Sept - J.F.Penn

It's interesting that you don't research while writing – I have so many tabs open as I write, researching constantly in first draft. It's the bit I enjoy the most… But you're better at dialog than me, better flow, which probably stems from not stopping so much.

23 Sept - J. Thorn

I have to shut everything down when I write. Any tab is a distraction and my ADD kills my word count.

28 Sept - J. Thorn

As we approach the end, I'm totally fine with you writing as much or as little of it as you want. Because it was your story idea, I want to honor the end like the beginning. As we've been doing, I'll follow your lead. Almost there...

30 Sept - J.Thorn

Writing was fast and furious today as it always is for me in the last stages of the first draft. I'm so excited to write my final scene tomorrow… I usually do 5-7 revisions before sending to an editor, but that's because I don't research or self-edit in first draft. I feel like this draft is worlds ahead of where my usual first drafts are, which is kind of the point of this collaborating stuff. I agree that this has been a smooth process and so much fun. For me, the first draft is the hardest part, so I have no doubt the editing will be easier.

1 Oct - J.F.Penn

I'm expecting to cycle through and add a layer to the whole thing in this pass, as well as sort out chapter flow. I've learned a lot about that – and ending on cliffhangers, not natural 'scene' endings.

On my own books, I'm pretty much down to one revision before edits now. But then I spend more time on that first draft, cycling through with the internet open for thesaurus lookups and detail on setting.

1 Oct - J.Thorn

HIGH FIVES!!!!!!!!!!!!!!!!!!!!!!!!!!!!!!!!!!!!!!! 59.5 thousand words of a damn good first draft in 19 days! Amazing… Really enjoying the feeling of accomplishment today.

3 Oct - J.F.Penn

I can really tell how you warmed up with your writing – the first chapters definitely need some rework. I started, but then decided that you'd better do your first pass before I have a go at it.

Being honest, I feel my control freakery emerging at this point.

It's uncomfortable to be reading stuff that I want to rewrite, but they are not my words, so I don't feel like I have the right. You also told me that you do a lot more drafts than I do, so I am fighting that urge, although I have done some stuff.

4 Oct - J.F.Penn

I'm feeling pretty control freakish about the edits and the final draft, to be honest.

I'm not sure about this lack of ego thing!

I want to handle it all now but I know I can't – and that's not the point.

4 Oct - J.Thorn

I seriously will not be upset if you edit out scenes I wrote. Honestly. We acknowledged you as the driver of this project, and as such, you need to drive. I've had your role before, which is why I understand the need to be a control freak on the edit. I always keep in mind that the goal of a collab is to produce the best story possible. Story trumps all, including egos.

5 Oct - J.F.Penn

Thank you - You're good at this. If we do another one together, a better outline that includes the polarity shift would be a good idea. And if you take the story lead next time, I will take your lead on edits.

[Explanatory note: The polarity shift is covered in Shawn Coyne's book, The Story Grid, *an essential for any author. You can also* listen to an interview with Shawn about the concept here.*]*

5 Oct - J.Thorn

I wanted to capture my feelings at this stage. I'm really excited. It's the same excitement as when I get a manuscript back from my editor. I know there is still a lot of work to be done, but the story now exists and it's a great feeling knowing I can share it with readers soon. I know you worry about your control-freakish tendencies, but as someone who has collaborated with others on several occasions, I've found working with you to be delightful. We established your leadership role and so I never felt slighted or jaded. In fact, I enjoyed following your lead, as I've been the driver in other collaborations. And I think we're taking for granted how different this story is.

We've created something new and unique, something better than either of us could have done on our own. I'm so pleased and I can't wait to hit publish on it. Well, for you to hit publish on it from your KDP dashboard.

8. What happens if it goes wrong?

A failure in this context, not just for co-writing and collaboration but for writing in general, is the inability to get to market. The idea creation is easy, but as ever, the implementation of the idea into a finished book is the challenge.

Collaborations probably fail more often than they succeed, but you generally only see the ones that make it to the finish line. It is important to recognize when problems occur and then make mutual decisions about whether or not to proceed. Sometimes it is better to end the partnership, provided both parties are honest and upfront as soon as possible.

There is nothing wrong with failure. The seeds of our growth and success are often in our greatest failures. So even if things do go wrong, don't let that put you off trying collaborations again. Both J. and Joanna have been in a number of projects that didn't make it very far or collapsed later in the process. You just get up, dust yourself off and move on to the next project.

> "The most important thing in deciding to do a collaboration is that you must have a prior relationship with someone. It doesn't have to be an in-person one, and it doesn't have to be extensive or long.
>
> But I've had at least 10 failed collaborations, and all of those failed because the people involved were acquaintances or cold-emailed me and I didn't really have a relationship with them. So a relation-

ship of some kind is the single most important element.

If that element is satisfied, if you have someone who you know and you trust and you're friends with, then set up a project that's small-scale and manageable, a short story or a novella and get the process down before doing a novel." - J. Thorn

Another important characteristic of any writer, especially in a collaboration, is persistence. Or, as entrepreneurs call it, grit. You must keep trying and failing until you find something that works. Your first collaboration might not make it to market, so it becomes important to figure out why and then try again.

What kind of things can go wrong?

Here are some examples so you can address them in your initial agreement:

- One writer dominates and the other feels put down or marginalized, or even bullied

- One writer does all the work and feels that the other one is not putting in enough time writing, word count or marketing help

- Life gets in the way and other priorities come up. One of the writers misses deadlines over and over again until the project is unsustainable

Some co-writing projects can end abruptly, like any human relationship can. But more often than not, they tend to fade away when deadlines come and go or when one writer is no longer interested in moving the project forward.

The best way to protect the co-writing project is to start

one on the foundation of an existing relationship. This lessens the risk of the collaboration failing and it makes it more likely you'll succeed. As in any relationship, communication is key. Whether you share a diary or have periodic Skype chats, keeping each other informed and being honest will prevent conflict.

In the end, there will be co-writing projects that will not make it to market, but if you are friends with your collaborator and you can help each other through your mutual anxieties, the project will be successful.

9. Other types of collaboration and co-creation

Of course, co-writing a book is just one way of collaborating in publishing. Indie authors are also using other models to work with other writers.

(1) Marketing collaborations: multi-author boxsets

Multi-author boxsets can be loosely defined as a collection of titles from multiple authors published by one author and sold as a single title ebook. Although these first appeared on Amazon, they can be created and sold on any digital book publishing platform.

The boxsets are usually genre specific, and each author contributes a title that has already been published in other formats. This technique is not usually done for paperbacks because of the high overhead of creating a book with thousands of pages and a physical box that must be shipped to a customer.

Multi-author boxsets require a great deal of management, which includes cover and 3D boxset design, publishing and marketing coordination as well as record-keeping and royalty disbursement over time.

Both of us have used multi-author boxsets successfully. J. Thorn managed the *This is the End* collection with help from Glynn James. The titles included were generally the first book in a series. Although strategies vary, the Thorn/James collections were priced at 99c to maximize discoverability at the sacrifice of royalties.

One Day in Budapest by J.F.Penn was included in the Deadly Dozen, a boxset with 12 thriller authors that sold over 110,000 copies and made the New York Times and USA Today bestseller lists. Again, the boxset was priced at 99c to maximize sales and marketing value, rather than royalties.

However, Amazon has been cracking down on the multi-author box set that includes titles individually enrolled in KDP Select. It is important to make sure you are not violating any distributor or retailer's terms of service before publishing a multi-author box set.

(2) Creative collaborations: 'World' sharing

A writer's world includes their settings, characters, plot lines and other aspects that relate to their books, and some authors open up their worlds for others to write in. However, this type of writing requires clear communication and copyright permissions, so proceed with caution.

They can be formalized such as Amazon's Kindle Worlds program (e.g. J. Thorn's *Vampire Apocalypse* in J.R. Rain's Samantha Moon World) or informal, where the authors agree to collaborate without using a platform like Kindle Worlds (e.g. J. Thorn's *Lost Track* short story in the world of *The Beam* – concept created by Sean Platt, written by J. Thorn and then revised by Sean Platt).

An author can grant another author permission to write and publish a title in their world without formal creative collaboration or marketing collaboration (e.g. J. Thorn's *Killer* short story in the world of Hugh Howey's *Half Way Home*).

10. Tips for multi-author boxsets

Joanna's book *One Day in Budapest* was part of a twelve-author boxset, *Deadly Dozen*, which hit the New York Times Bestseller list for two weeks, and the New York Times list for six weeks in March 2014.

Why do a multi-author boxset anyway?

Boxsets represent amazing value for customers, as they get multiple books for a lower price, which is why they are so popular. Deadly Dozen featured 12 books from 12 award-winning and bestselling thriller authors, with over 600 five-star reviews on Amazon and a saving of over US$40.

Traditional publishers have been doing boxsets in print for years, and they have become popular amongst indies for ebook bundling as a marketing tactic, cross-pollinating readers and boosting email lists.

Boxsets can be great opportunities for authors to collaborate with other authors to reach a different audience, or maximize point of sale revenue from one customer with their own series or theme boxset. While the 'rules' of the New York Times list have been changed to disallow multi-author boxsets, they can still be an effective marketing tactic.

Here are the top things Joanna learned in the process of doing the boxset:

(1) Collaboration and relationships are the most important thing

The Deadly Dozen was a fantastic joint promotion effort, made possible because 12 authors plus a brilliant coordinator worked together to achieve a specific goal. There have been other boxsets by romance authors that have made the New York Times list, so we knew it was possible. It was a case of all pulling together at the same time.

We all pitched our lists on different days, we all paid for promotional activities, collectively we paid for advertising and prizes, we all used social media to spread the word and we asked for shout-outs from other long-term author friends. Everyone pitched in and took time out of their schedules to make this happen within a specific time period.

This is not out of reach for you to do as well. When I was starting out, I didn't have any author friends. I didn't know anyone and I didn't have any web presence or social media following or email list. We all have to start somewhere.

Authentic relationships take time to build, so don't expect to just email a few people and go from there. I started on Twitter, then met people through podcast interviews, and then in person at conventions/conferences like London Book Fair and Thrillerfest.

I'm an introvert (as many of you are), so these things are hard for me. I still have heart palpitations before I get on Skype to interview people. I still have to psych myself up for live events. But it's worth it!

(2) You need sales in more than one store to hit the lists

You can't be exclusive on Amazon KDP Select and hit the bestseller lists. Even if you sell 200,000 copies in one day on Amazon alone, you won't make it. It's important to have sales through at least one other store – iBooks, Nook, Kobo as well as Amazon, even if the numbers are smaller because the lists measure across sites.

This is a challenge, as the other sites generally work on human-selected merchandising rather than an algorithm that doesn't discriminate between traditional publishing and indie. But if you focus on growing your audience on other platforms over time, you can manage this.

(3) Decide on the goal before the marketing campaign starts

Related to the point above, if our goal had been to get to #1 on just Amazon.com, we would have gone about it in a different way, e.g. with one big spike in the marketing plan. But the wonderful Diane Capri had the foresight to focus on the New York Times and USA Today lists, so everything was geared towards that goal and involved more of a stepped approach over a longer period. A lot of our general author marketing is just aimed at 'selling more books,' but perhaps it is time to get more specific.

(4) Building your email list should always be the highest priority

As an individual, it's difficult to hit the lists, as we all have smaller reach alone. But it can clearly be done, as indie romance authors H.M. Ward and Bella Andre hit the NY

Times list regularly, through a combination of huge email lists, merchandising and promotional spikes. It's just a case of building up that list slowly over time, by delivering quality books that readers want more of, for years. But hey, what else would you rather be doing than writing?

Postscript: Is it worth trying to hit the lists anyway?

Many authors would like to 'get their letters,' but it has become much harder to do in recent years and it has always been a game.

> "No bestseller list measures the actual bestselling books. Every single bestseller list either measures a limited number of sales in a few places, or far worse, it's a curated list and a small group of people are deciding what to put on their list. And they're picking books based on what they think are important books, not based on what they are actually selling." - *Tucker Max, Entrepreneur magazine*

In January 2017, the New York Times removed their ebook lists, along with a number of other bestseller lists like graphic novels and mass market paperbacks, so it has become skewed towards physical hardback sales in specific bookstores in America, with little to do with volume sales.

In March 2017, mega-bestselling romance author Marie Force wrote a blog post about the day she stopped chasing the bestseller lists. It had become an addiction that made her life a rollercoaster.

> "I was gaming a system that doesn't really matter (in the grand scheme of things) at the expense of my customers—you know, the lovely readers who actually BUY my books! *#&^@^ MADNESS!"

Kristine Kathryn Rusch, author and editor of hundreds of books, describes the "trajectory of obsession and disillusionment" that accompanies this desire to hit the bestseller lists. She says it took her years to get over her bestseller list obsession but now, she says:

> "My business is based on a lot of product, published wide in a worldwide market, using print, audio, ebook, translations, and more. I don't usually look at an individual book's ranking in one format in one marketplace—and even though Amazon is the biggest marketplace at the moment, it's certainly not the only one."

Of course, if it is your goal to hit the New York Times or USA Today lists, it's still possible, but you'll need a coordinated marketing strategy for a book that fits the specific requirements of the lists, and that is beyond the scope of this book.

11. Tips for managing a 10-author collaboration

These are J. Thorn's top tips after managing *The Black Fang Betrayal,* a ten-author collaborative novel.

To say it was a logistical challenge would be an understatement. Spanning ten months and several continents, *The Black Fang Betrayal* is a tale of mystery and suspense, described as "The Sopranos with warlocks." Every writer brought a unique style and voice, and yet a single, cohesive story emerged.

There are two key points worth considering before discussing specifics. This project proved to me that there is too much emphasis placed on 'the meeting' and its significance in the collaborative process. Being an introvert, I prefer written communication. Because I was the project manager for *The Black Fang Betrayal*, I decided we were not going to meet physically while working on the project.

Everything we accomplished, from the original concept to the marketing plan for the book launch, was done through email and a private Facebook group. We did not use conference calls, webinars, Hangouts or any other method of synchronous communication. This type of collaboration is more about management than writing, and as you will see, organization is essential for this type of project.

I believe that if a novel can be written this way, just about any collaboration can be successful using the best practices of project management. Here are my lessons:

(1) It will take longer than you think

There will be issues and setbacks.

People will leave the project while others will join the group. Technology will fail. Someone will get angry. Someone will ignore your emails.

All of this means it's essential to allow plenty of time and make the deadlines artificially short. You will likely incur costs upfront and if you can, it's best to have the funds saved and set aside rather than asking the participants for money. You can reimburse yourself from royalties later. Notice that there is a bit of a risk, in that you may not ultimately earn enough to recoup your initial costs, so never use funds you're not willing or able to lose completely.

(2) Keep moving forward

A delicate balance exists between planning for obstacles and enforcing deadlines. You have to do both. However, it's important that all participants feel as though the project is constantly moving forward. This pace may eventually force one or more members to drop out, but you'll be able to find others who are comfortable with the momentum.

Deadlines force a sense of urgency and also hold everyone accountable. Early on in the project, you will get a sense of which participants will meet the deadlines and which ones will not. Be kind and gracious, and remember that we all need a little space. Be firm with the deadlines and be persistent in asking for what you need, but do it with a light touch.

(3) Expect rejection

Your invitation, proposal or pitch will be rejected more times than it is accepted. In fact, some of your invitations will be ignored completely. You may have to ask five to ten times more people just to reach the minimum you need to make the project happen. This is natural and is by no means a reflection on you. People are extremely busy and highly skeptical, especially if the project you're proposing is unique or different. If someone declines, be respectful and move on.

If your invitation is not answered in 48 hours, move on.

The initial communication with a prospective collaborator is important, because it provides insight on their work habits. Early email responders tend to be early with deadlines and meet all expectations as well. This is not a judgment, but merely an observation on human behavior in the workplace. As long as the return communication reaches you within what you consider to be a reasonable response window, accept that person into your collaboration.

When you are pitching or asking for participation, make saying "yes" as easy as possible. Provide all of the relevant information upfront and keep it up to date. Rather than including the information in a single correspondence, post it in the Cloud or on a private web page for prospective participants to view easily. This ensures you can always keep the information current for everyone.

Don't make people fill out unnecessary forms or ask them for answers to open-ended questions. Your goal in the pitch is to get a "yes," so make it simple. Once a participant agrees to be part of your collaboration, give them an out as late as possible in the process.

Someone might be initially excited about the project but then less so as it veers away from their initial understanding. Allow for a graceful exit.

At some point in the process, it should be made clear (in a written contract) that participants cannot leave the collaboration after a certain date or timeframe, but also understand that people can and will need to opt out due to special circumstances.

Make sure to clearly state the minimum level of involvement required by each participant to be a part of the collaboration (such as the minimum word count in the case of *The Black Fang Betrayal*), but also encourage motivated participants to do more.

Prospective collaborators should have only two major deadlines: signing on to your project and submitting a final draft. You will need other items from them along the way, but it helps to frame the scope for collaborators while making it easy for them to participate.

(4) You must lead

As the project manager or the idea generator, you should be passionate about your project. Other people will be excited about it, too. However, it's natural for the person running the project to be the most invested in its success. At times, you will have to rely on your own passion and motivation to carry the project forward. In order to excite others, you need to be clear in your vision and in how you communicate that vision with the group.

For *The Black Fang Betrayal*, I structured the collaboration and told each prospective author what would be required of them, providing information on character, setting, genre and plot. Remember, you are asking them to join your collaboration, to follow your lead. If they say "yes," it means they want to be led and are willing to follow you. Take that responsibility seriously, but also be aware that decisions by committee can often lead to a mediocre result as everyone tries to find a safe middle ground. Not everyone will agree with every decision you make, but if you are clear in your vision and lead with confidence, they will trust and support you.

I hope to improve my leadership skills on my next collaboration. In this one, I neglected to specify the time of the year when the story took place and I didn't require the final drafts to be formatted in any particular fashion, which meant I had to spend extra time fixing those inconsistencies prior to publication.

(5) You must listen

This element of project management is the most difficult to articulate because it comes down to feel. Although your vision must be clear and you should lead with confidence, there will be times when you must solicit feedback from the team.

Input is invaluable and ignoring it can be catastrophic. It is not necessary to sit and speak to someone face-to-face to solicit feedback. Meetings, in the traditional sense, are not necessary. Clear and timely communication is essential.

When possible, try to structure your questions. For example, rather than asking for open-ended ideas on a particular aspect of the collaboration, give your team two or three choices. Do this in a group setting (such as through a private Facebook group or closed bulletin board) so you can get a sense of the group dynamic.

Email is not beneficial in a collaboration of this type, because it puts the conversation in silos. You should use email only to deliver important information to the participants, and expect that communication to be mostly one-way. Because group communication requires a different kind of effort than a traditional face-to-face meeting, participants are more likely to be on task and can contribute when they're most attentive rather than trying to force interest on a specified day and time.

(6) You must be organized

It is impossible to lead a collaboration of any type without being organized.

Repeat. It is impossible to lead a collaboration of any type without being organized!

Although technical issues will always arise, today's technology allows greater and more seamless organization than ever before. Through Cloud-based solutions and shared documents, you can keep the project organized from just about anywhere, from any device. Technological tools aside, it is essential to have solid personal organization.

If you are not naturally inclined toward organization, you may not be ready to manage a collaboration. However, organization is a learned skill and there is no shortage of resources available for a person who wants to become more efficient and organized. Being organized means utilizing systems (such as iCloud, Google Drive, DropBox, Trello, etc.) in addition to maintaining accurate records. You should keep a spreadsheet of deadlines, save all emails and messages sent to participants, develop a launch plan and more.

Save everything you create in a logical folder system and make sure that folder system is in the Cloud or backed up (nightly) to another location. In today's computing environment, there is no excuse for losing files in a computer crash, and nothing will kill your project faster. If that happens, your participants will be frustrated and lose confidence in you and may be less likely to help you pick up the pieces.

Avoid the use of paper, because it makes it hard on participants. For example, rather than using a fax machine to have participants sign a contract, use a free online document signing site like Docracy. With a free, registered account, contracts are signed through a web browser without the need to print and physically return the document.

Remember, you are the project manager and the one most passionate about your project, so you should shoulder most of the responsibility. Your goal should be to make the process as easy as possible for your collaborators.

(7) Enforce structure but do it gently

No matter how passionate, clear, organized and decisive you are as a project manager, there will always be issues that threaten to derail the collaboration. Obstacles will appear that you never anticipated. Frustrations will mount and you will be tempted to give up. This is a natural part of the process. If you're utilizing the systems you have in place, and if you're motivated to continue, you can keep things on schedule.

There will be missed deadlines and misinterpretations. Use a gentle hand to recalibrate and remember that you are dealing with humans. We are all complex, emotional and sometimes irrational creatures. Keep it all in perspective and keep it moving forward. In the end, you'll be glad you did.

I'm thrilled with *The Black Fang Betrayal* and I wish you success on your own collaboration.

12. Thoughts on a co-writing project with four authors

In March 2017, four authors boarded the 8.05pm train from Chicago to New Orleans and then spent a week in the Big Easy writing the dark fantasy story that became *American Demon Hunters: Sacrifice*. The four authors were: J.F.Penn (Joanna), J. Thorn, Zach Bohannon, and Lindsay Buroker, established authors with over 100 books between them in various different genres, but all with some aspect of fantasy.

The idea

J. Thorn came up with the idea of writing a book together on a train and emailed the other authors six months prior to the trip. J. had collaborated with J.F.Penn on *Risen Gods,* and separately with Zach Bohannon on a number of other projects. J. and Zach were friends but had never met before, J. and Joanna had never met before, despite knowing each other for years online. Joanna and Lindsay had met in person once at a conference but mainly knew each other from the online indie community.

> "There's something magical about train travel. I really believe that. It's romantic. Romantic in the sense of the history of travel, not in, like, lovey romantic! *[Note from Joanna: Those sleeper compartments were not romantic!]* I've taken trips from

Chicago to California and back multiple times on Amtrak. And for this one, I thought that the destination really mattered. I had been to New Orleans a few times. It's one of my favorite cities in the world." - J. Thorn

"I was actually sold on the idea of the trip probably more than the collaboration. J. Thorn emailed me and said, 'Hey, we're gonna fly to Chicago, take an overnight train to New Orleans and then hang out there and write.' It's a great city. I thought it really sounded like a fun adventure. These were things I hadn't done before." - Lindsay Buroker

"It just seemed like too good of an opportunity to be able to travel with three other writers and have this joint experience together. At the end of the week, we had a first draft of a book, but for me, it's been more about the friendships that we've built over the week and learning from each other. It's so unique and I didn't want to miss out on that." - Zach Bohannon

"I've wanted to visit New Orleans for a long time and so this was a great excuse to finally go. I've found ideas for another book in my own ARKANE series as well as co-writing *Sacrifice*, so it's been fantastic for writing at the same time as scratching my travel itch." - J.F.Penn

There was a certain level of trust between the authors because of knowing each other, at least online, beforehand. We also had respect for the level of professionalism we all brought to the project. There was no doubt that we could each write our fair share of words for the story.

Planning before Chicago

We had a Skype call before everyone booked their flights to discuss the practicalities. Joanna had to fly from London, England so it was important to be sure the project would go ahead before significant financial investment. We used a shared Google Drive and various documents to write everything down and made sure all the financial and legal copyright questions were answered early on. We decided to wait until we were physically together before plotting the story, but one author in particular struggled with waiting …

> "My writing process always starts with research and my fiction emerges from the real world. I couldn't get on that train without something concrete to base a story on. So I spent a day in Chicago looking for something to spark ideas. I visited the International Museum of Surgical Science and discovered a 4000 year old Peruvian skull with a hole drilled in it to let the demons out. Since I'd read the other American Demon Hunter stories, I knew this could be an interesting hook for our story. I came up with a character, a British relic thief, to fit the skull, before I met the others and just hoped they would accept the premise." - J.F.Penn

The Peruvian skull did indeed become the center of the story and it was actually good to have an initial idea that we could all write around, rather than spending time coming up with something on the train which would have taken more time. Instead, we could brainstorm how the story would work around the skull. Joanna also read everything in the American Demon Hunters world and wrote notes on aspects that would resonate with the other stories. This provided other plot ideas that we took further as a group in our story meetings.

On the 8.05pm train from Chicago to New Orleans

Joanna and Lindsay had a few hours at the train station together and, inevitably, discussed story ideas. Both wanted to set the book on the train itself, which would give the story pacing and a clear reason for the characters to stay together. J. and Zach had thought the book would be set in New Orleans, but they quickly agreed to keep the story on the train, adding pacing and a time limit to the adventure.

We decided upfront that we would each write one character point-of-view and stay with that character throughout. This meant minimal confusion for the reader and it meant we could maintain our own writing voices. If you read *Sacrifice*, it's possible to discern who wrote which character if you've read other works by the authors. Each character has a representative symbol as well.

This has been different compared to J.'s other collaborations. In *Risen Gods*, we both wrote various chapters and then edited it into one voice, which is similar to how Zach and J. have written before. But because of the constrained time period, and because of the maturity of the various authors involved, we decided to write with individual voices in *Sacrifice* and only light edit for story rather than voice. This is definitely a more advanced form of collaboration that would be harder for authors who aren't that confident in their writing voice as yet.

The opening scenes of the story came together as we all experienced the train journey. The details of the sleeper carriages, the food, the constant horn blaring, and the layout of the cars themselves were informed by our trip. Even our conductor, Patrick, made it into the story – although he might not have made it all the way to New Orleans …

In New Orleans

When we arrived, we checked into a hotel on the edge of the French Quarter. We had a story meeting after breakfast and then met again before dinner to discuss the scenes for the next day. We wrote our scenes in Google Docs in the shared Google Drive.

We attempted to order the scenes during the week, but it soon proved difficult to manage the movement of each of our characters on the train without writing overlapping scenes. This was one of the main challenges and something we tried to address by talking a lot. We had several story meetings a day, one around breakfast and then one at dinner. We also had a WhatsApp group so we could message each other on status as well as encouragement.

By Tuesday night, we had an outline for the rest of the story and the meetings consisted of the detail around those scenes and some choreography as to where each character was at specific times.

"The compressed timeframe, the logistical pieces, and the time element made this challenging. We've been working a lot this week. Between the reading and the writing and the story meetings, it hasn't just been a vacation. The creative process is also messy. There are moments where it's really smooth and moments where it's hard. One of my challenges is the time element. I don't always read as carefully as I should because I'm worried about getting the words in. That caused me to write a few things that wound up getting cut, and that's okay. There's a human element to it, too. Tuesday night was the low point and we were all exhausted and it was late. That was the moment where the end seemed so far away. You have that excitement at the beginning and then you hit that middle point where it just feels hard." - *J. Thorn*

"I imagine if we did it again with the same group of people, it would be a lot smoother because now, we know what our needs and preferences are. Early on, I thought it wasn't going to work, that we would end up with an actual train wreck. But now I think, overall, I'm almost a little surprised. I think we're going to end up with a cohesive story." - *Lindsay Buroker, speaking on the Thursday in New Orleans before the first draft was finished.*

We also had some fun times in New Orleans, visiting the original House of the Rising Sun as well as the Museum of Death and eating a lot of southern food. Beignets and cafe-au-lait make for a great writing sugar rush!

"We're all introverts and generally spend a lot of time alone. I was apprehensive about some perceived requirement to be social, but we all found our own rhythm. We mostly wrote alone in cafes, although Zach and J. did write in the same one sometimes. I did a lot of tourist stuff (otherwise known as book research!) by myself, but it was also really great to do some things together.

Lindsay and I did an airboat adventure in the bayou together, and all four of us went on a walking tour around the French Quarter led by two other writers, Laura and Dan Martone. We also had dinners together and talked about writing things as well as life stuff. It was actually brilliant to spend time with other creatives with no judgment around topic of conversation. Because let's face it, who else can you discuss murder weapons and Amazon algorithms with?" - *J.F.Penn*

Back home: The editing and production process

Joanna took the first pass on a complete edit, catering to her control freakish tendencies and her writing style of cutting a lot of scenes and characters together, which is a common element of thriller fiction. She copied and pasted the scenes out of the Google Drive into Scrivener and then hacked them apart and stitched them back together so the characters presented the sequential story to the reader without overlapping detail. At this stage, the manuscript became known as Frankenstein and it was pretty ugly. Joanna edits by hand, so she printed the whole thing out and spent several days reworking it, attempting to maintain balance between the voices as well as bring coherence to the plot.

Then the manuscript when through the other writers, J. first, followed by Zach and then Lindsay. J. was particularly concerned with harmonizing the language used for the train as each writer had used different terminology. He developed a glossary and updated elements in his edit.

> "We have four different point of view characters and so we're each able to write our own scenes through that character's eyes. It actually makes a lot of sense that they would have very different voices as different people.
>
> Something we're going to have to address in the edits is when our characters interact with each other. You look at dialogue that other people have written for your character and you're like, 'oh please, what is that?' So we'll have to change that in the edits. I think we're all being flexible about that. Nobody is saying, 'you can't touch my work or change what my character said.'" - *Lindsay Buroker,*

speaking on the Thursday in New Orleans before the first draft was finished.

As we had four professional authors editing the story, we just used a proofreader for the final pass before publication. Joanna then formatted the ebook with Vellum, adding the symbols per character and the back matter. J. published it.

Marketing for the book

We had a specific meeting towards the end of the week to discuss marketing. On the plus side, we're all established authors, so we have readers waiting for our books and we all have a mailing list and social media followers.

But on the flip side, each of us has a *different* audience and many readers will not stray outside the established series they enjoy.

Combining parts of our audience for this book would likely result in messy 'also-boughts,' and confuse the algorithms that rely on data to recommend books to readers.

> "Even as late as 2016, the general mindset was that you had a book launch and you went far and wide with the message. You just blasted everyone you possibly could and played the percentages.
>
> But then Chris Fox outlined how data science impacted the algorithms and how confusing your readership could result in *fewer* sales. It's actually better to only tell a targeted group of genre specific readers about your launch, and once you have trained the algorithms, then go wide. But that wasn't possible in this launch, so we just decided to go for the all-out-blast approach!" - *J. Thorn*

NOTE: You can watch/listen/read an interview with Chris Fox on how to use data science to sell more books here: www.TheCreativePenn.com/data

In the end, we decided to ignore any impact on the algorithms and just launch as widely as possible, using bribery in launch week to get our existing readers to buy and to tap into the wider author community.

For one week only, we decided that the formatted ebook would contain launch bonuses, including extra fiction and non-fiction, as well as chances to win First Edition paperbacks with a limited edition signed photo of the four of us, plus an opportunity to win a podcast slot and a consulting session with the author of choice. We figured this was a good deal for a few dollars!

At the end of the launch week, we would upload a new ebook version without those bonus pages, which would give people an incentive to buy and (hopefully), push the book up the charts.

Lessons Learned

There was never any doubt that we would finish this project. We told our audiences about it and we all had too much invested for it to fail. The final story was a true collaboration and we're all happy with it. In terms of lessons learned, the biggest one would be to have a much clearer outline with character choreography before rushing into writing. A story bible for the existing American Demon Hunters world would also have been useful. So basically, more prep work!

> "This has been the most challenging collaboration but also the most rewarding, because this happened in real time. If you're doing a collaboration

asynchronously and you don't have a definite deadline, you have the luxury of stretching things out and rethinking them.

There are always deadlines, but for *Sacrifice*, we knew going in that we have this many days, this many minutes together. We designed it this way, but this one has been intense. We had to get things done and couldn't obsess over too much. We had to compromise with each other over our story ideas, over the cover, the title, even the marketing ideas and only fight for the elements we really cared about, which for all of us, was our characters.

If I did a similar project again, I would give it a genre theme. If all the writers already wrote in the genre and knew the conventions, it would be a much more streamlined process. I would also do more groundwork beforehand. We made the decision not to this time and that was exciting. But doing it again, I would probably do more upfront work so that we could hit the ground running at the start." *J. Thorn*

Would we do it again?

"I collaborate a lot and I'm always looking for new and different ways to do it, because I like a challenge. So I do some things the same way, but I like to try and up my game and just try something different and really push myself. This week has been the most invigorating and yet challenging collaboration I've ever done. And I would do it again in a heartbeat." - *J. Thorn*

"You always have to continue to try to grow as a writer, even though you have a lot of books out and you've been doing pretty well. It's good to keep pushing yourself and try different things. As a natural introvert, to do something with other people has been interesting and a learning experience, as cheesy as that sounds. I know other people don't write the way I do, and I've always known that, but this has been a growth experience, to try and work with others with different styles and write in a different genre and try to bring it all together.

This will be something I'll remember always and the whole experience has been very unique. It was a challenging first collaboration but probably a lot more fun than just uploading documents into Dropbox from across the world with another author." - *Lindsay Buroker*

Read the book

American Demon Hunters: Sacrifice is available now in ebook, print and audiobook formats:

www.JFPenn.com/sacrifice

Want more behind the scenes?

The four authors were interviewed on a number of podcasts during the week in New Orleans, including Joanna's Creative Penn Podcast. For a behind-the-scenes experience, you can listen/watch or read the transcript of the interviews: www.TheCreativePenn.com/4authors

You can also see behind-the-scenes pictures of the authors here on Pinterest:

www.pinterest.com/jfpenn/american-demon-hunters-sacrifice/

Are you interested in collaboration and co-writing?

J. Thorn and Zach Bohannon are providing resources for authors looking to co-write. Check out: www.theauthorcopilot.com/retreat for more information.

Afterword

So, with all we've learned about co-writing, would we do it again?

It's a definite yes from both of us and in fact, we did do it again! *Risen Gods* came out in 2015, and in 2017, we co-wrote *American Demon Hunters: Sacrifice*, along with Lindsay and Zach.

J. and Zach are starting their own publishing company, with the aim to do a lot more collaborations. Joanna is already co-writing with several other authors on new projects. Collaboration and co-writing has become ever more possible in a fast-moving indie world where creatives can get together and produce books faster. We believe that this will be an option for an increasing number of indie authors in the years to come, especially as tools emerge to make the process of co-creation much easier.

We wish you all the best for your own collaboration and co-creation!

Risen Gods

Here's the result of J. Thorn and J.F.Penn's original co-writing experience, *Risen Gods*, available in ebook, print and audiobook formats.

> *"It doesn't matter what you believe. The time is here regardless. They are coming. After so long, the gods are rising again."*

Ben Henare turned away from the gods of his ancestors to follow his own path, choosing the modern world over myths of demons and monsters.

But when New Zealand is shaken by earthquakes and dark powers are released, Ben must fight his way north through ice caves and oceans, battling the evil god Whiro and the creatures of the earth and sky.

Lucy Campion is a trainee doctor, a rational scientist with no belief in demons. When her parents are killed and her sister is threatened, Lucy is tasked with carrying an ancient talisman north to where the oceans meet. But both human and supernatural foes stand in her way.

As the people they love are threatened and New Zealand begins to crumble, can Ben and Lucy find each other again and save the country from the wrath of the Risen Gods?

Risen Gods is a fast-paced, urban fantasy adventure set in Aotearoa/New Zealand, rich with Maori mythology of gods and goddesses, demons and devils. If you enjoy supernatural thrillers, download a sample or buy now.

From New York Times and USA Today bestselling supernatural thriller author J.F.Penn, and dark fantasy author, J. Thorn, comes a stand-alone novel of demons, monsters, and Risen Gods.

Available now in ebook, print and audiobook formats at: www.JFPenn.com/risengods

American Demon Hunters: Sacrifice

Here's the result of the Four Authors on a Train co-writing experience, *American Demon Hunters: Sacrifice.*

A relic thief.

An ex-military Mom.

A grief stricken father willing to do anything to save his son.

An American Demon Hunter.

All aboard the 8.05 p.m. from Chicago to New Orleans for 19 hours that will change their lives.

When the relic of an ancient blood cult is used to summon the dead and open a portal to the beyond, demons escape onto the train. As the body count rises, each must fight to save their own lives and those of the people they love. New friendships are forged in the battles and love blossoms in the carnage.

But who will have to pay the ultimate sacrifice?

A dark fantasy story from four bestselling authors who just happened to be on the 8.05pm from Chicago one March evening …

Find out more or buy the book: www.JFPenn.com/sacrifice

Appendix 1: Example agreement

⁂ Note: This is an example only and was not drafted by an attorney. The user accepts full responsibility and recognizes that neither Joanna Penn nor J. Thorn is liable for any losses incurred from the use of the form.⁂

COLLABORATION AGREEMENT

THIS AGREEMENT, made on <date> , between [name and address] (hereinafter "PRODUCER"), and [name and address] (hereinafter "COLLABORATOR"), with respect to the production of the novel collaboration hereinafter the "WORK"), to be published by PRODUCER.

In consideration of the mutual promises contained herein, and for other good and valuable consideration, receipt of which is hereby acknowledged, the parties agree as follows:

1. The copyright in the WORK shall be jointly registered and held in the names of both PRODUCER and COLLABORATOR.

2. Credits in the WORK shall read: "Written by COLLABORATOR and PRODUCER; Published by COLLABORATOR and PRODUCER," and the names shall be written on all credits.

3. Royalties from the publication (in all forms including ebook, audiobook and paperback) of the WORK and from the disposition of any subsidiary rights therein

(including but not limited to films, television, video games and merchandising) shall be divided as follows: 50% for COLLABORATOR and 50% for PRODUCER. Publication costs (including but not limited to editing, cover design, proofreading) shall be paid equally by PRODUCER and COLLABORATOR.

4. The complete publication and sale of the WORK shall remain the right of PRODUCER who is the only authorized publisher with royalty structure stated in paragraph 3 above. PRODUCER may transfer publication right to COLLABORATOR, in writing.

5. No agreement for the publication of the WORK or for the disposition of any of the subsidiary rights therein shall be valid without the signature of both PRODUCER and COLLABORATOR. However, either party may grant a written power of attorney to the other setting forth the specific conditions under which the power may be exercised.

6. All agreements for publication and disposition of any subsidiary rights in the WORK shall provide that each party's share shall be paid directly to him.

7. All subsequent rights to a sequel or derivative piece to the WORK (hereinafter the "SEQUEL") including the world of the WORK, belong to PRODUCER and COL-LABORATOR under the same terms and conditions of the WORK, including but not limited to WORK title, domain name and accompanying graphic art. Individual, derivative works permissible only with written permission of PRODUCER and COLLABORATOR.

(i) Unless mutually agreed in advance by PRODUCER and COLLABORATOR, THIRD PARTY shall not own any copyright, trademark or other rights in and to the WORK and/or any SEQUEL. All rights in and to the SEQUELS shall remain the sole property of PRODUCER. Any contribution of THIRD PARTY to a SEQUEL shall be done as a work-made-for-hire to the fullest extent permitted by law, and to the extent that such contribution is not considered a work-made-for-hire authored by PRODUCER in any jurisdiction, THIRD PARTY shall assign any and all rights he may have in the SEQUEL to PRODUCER.

8. Each party agrees not to violate copyright or any other law in the creation of the WORK. If it shall be found or claimed that the WORK violates an existing copyright, throughout the world, the party which created that portion of the WORK shall indemnify and hold harmless the other party.

9. This agreement shall continue in perpetuity. This agreement shall inure to the benefit of, and shall be binding upon, the heirs, executors, administrators, successors and assigns of the parties. This agreement shall be construed and enforced in accordance with the laws of the State of Ohio. This full agreement between the parties regarding the WORK, any amendments must be signed by all parties.

Should any party retain counsel for the purpose of enforcing its rights under this agreement against another party, then the prevailing party in any action commenced with regard to such dispute shall be entitled to receive from the other party payment or reimbursement of all costs and attorneys' fees reasonably incurred with respect thereto.

IN WITNESS WHEREOF, the parties hereto have signed this agreement as of [date].

From J. Thorn

"My mother-in-law published her first book at age 65 and I helped her do it. I can help you, too."

You've just finished writing your novel and now you can sit back while the royalties roll in, right?

WRONG.

Millions of books are for sale on Amazon. MILLIONS. Writing an incredible story is not enough. You need to know how to get a stunning cover, upload your book to the digital shelves, set up your author pages, write an engaging product description and more.

Need a writing coach or dedicated, individualized support?

J. Thorn is offering a very limited number of private coaching sessions for authors. Get help at:

www.theauthorcopilot.com

About J. Thorn

J. Thorn is a Top 100 Most Popular Author in Horror, Science Fiction, Action & Adventure and Fantasy (Amazon Author Rank). He has published over one million words and has sold more than 175,000 books worldwide. In March of 2014 Thorn held the #5 position in Horror alongside his childhood idols Dean Koontz and Stephen

King (at #4 and #2 respectively). He is an official, active member of the Horror Writers Association and a member of the Great Lakes Association of Horror Writers. J. is a contributor to disinformation.com and a staff writer for HeavyPlanet.net as well as a founding board member of the Author Marketing Institute.

Thorn earned a B.A. in American History from the University of Pittsburgh and an M.A. from Duquesne University. He has spent the last twenty years researching mysticism and the occult in colonial American history.

Get a free digital gift box from J. Thorn, which includes a novel, shorts, audio shorts and more: http://bit.ly/risen-gods

About Joanna Penn

Joanna Penn, writing as J.F.Penn, is a New York Times and USA Today bestselling author of thrillers and dark fiction, as well as writing inspirational non-fiction. Joanna is an international professional speaker and award-winning entrepreneur. She lives in Bath, England with her husband and enjoys a nice G&T.

Joanna's award-winning site for writers www.TheCreative-Penn.com helps people to write, publish and market their books through articles, audio, video and online products as well as live workshops. She is available internationally for speaking events aimed at writers, authors and entrepreneurs/small businesses. Joanna also has a popular weekly podcast for writers, The Creative Penn

Fiction writing site: www.JFPenn.com

Need help with writing, self-publishing or book marketing?

Get your free Author Blueprint, plus email course and video training:

www.TheCreativePenn.com/blueprint

Non-fiction Books for Authors

How to Market a Book

How to Make a Living with your Writing

Business for Authors:
How to be an Author Entrepreneur

Successful Self-Publishing

Co-writing a Book:
Collaboration and Co-creation for Writers

Public Speaking for Authors,
Creatives and Other Introverts

Career Change: Stop Hating your Job,
Discover What you Really Want to do and Start Doing it!

Multimedia courses for authors

How to Write a Novel:
From Idea to First Draft to Finished Manuscript

Creative Freedom:
How to make a living with your writing

Thriller novels writing as J.F.Penn

The ARKANE conspiracy thriller series:

Stone of Fire #1
Crypt of Bone #2
Ark of Blood #3
One Day In Budapest #4
Day of the Vikings #5
Gates of Hell #6
One Day in New York #7
Destroyer of Worlds #8
End of Days #9

If you like **crime thrillers with an edge of the supernatural**, join Detective Jamie Brooke and museum researcher Blake Daniel, in the London Psychic trilogy:

Desecration #1
Delirium #2
Deviance #3

If you enjoy **dark fantasy,** check out:

Risen Gods
American Demon Hunters: Sacrifice

A Thousand Fiendish Angels:
Short stories based on Dante's Inferno

More books coming soon.

You can sign up to be notified of new releases, giveaways and pre-release specials - plus, get a free book!

www.JFPenn.com/free

Printed in Great Britain
by Amazon